Written by
Lucy Pearce

Illustrated by
Adam Mason

Meet Joobi the Alien. Joobi is on a quest to help his human friends be happy. He brings them cake, balloons and books if they feel sad.

Joobi and his friends often sing, they do colouring and talk about everything.
Joobi's friends love it when he dances too, he morphs into a cow and says "MOOOOOOO".

There is just one human Joobi can't make happy, no matter how much he is super wacky. And his name is Noah…

Meet Noah, Noah lives at home with his mum. Noah was not happy and was making bad choices.

One day, he pushed his plate away and shouted loudly "I'm not hungry!"
Noahs mum gasped and said "Noah you love pancakes, why wont you eat?" Noah stayed silent and left his seat.

At school in the classroom, Noah struggled to listen. Noah complained that his stomach ached, he even refused Miss Jubilee's cake.

Noah could not understand why he was feeling so sad.

It was on one gloomy day, where Noah started to call for joobi.
Joobi Flew down with a playful "WOOO" but saw that Noah was weeping so he said "hey Noah, are you ok?"

Noah weeped and said "it makes me sad that i am so bad."
Joobi gasped and said "Noah, your not a bad human! You are a GOOD human who has just had some bad feelings!"
Noah looked up confused.

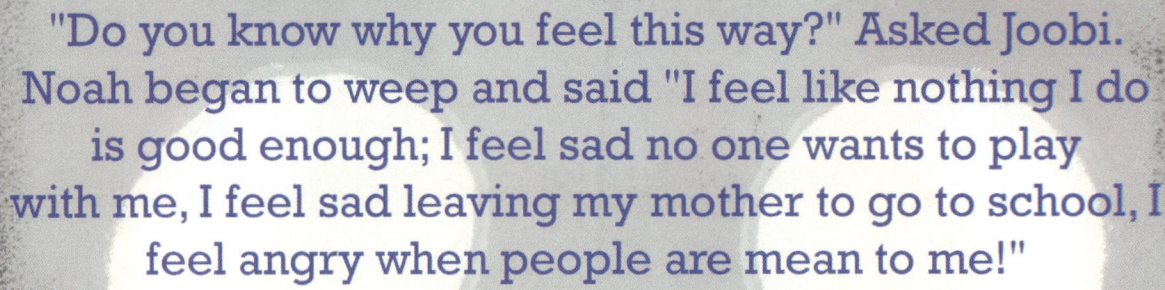

"Do you know why you feel this way?" Asked Joobi. Noah began to weep and said "I feel like nothing I do is good enough; I feel sad no one wants to play with me, I feel sad leaving my mother to go to school, I feel angry when people are mean to me!"

"I'm sorry you feel this way my friend, if you can't help the way you feel, its important you speak to someone so that you can heal" Joobi said with sympathy.

Joobi showed Noah a picture of a rotten flower and said "The flower looks rotten with its dark petals; because it has not been watered or looked after."

Joobi showed Noah another picture, but this time of a beautiful flower. "Can you see what is different about this flower?" Asked Joobi. "Its being watered?" Said Noah
"YES!" Joobi cheered, "You see if we look after our emotions just like this person is looking after this flower, we can grow and blossom into something wonderful."

Noah cheered up very much, but he soon realised it was time to go home. So they flew back into Noahs garden where Noahs mum was waiting for him. "Mum, im sorry I've been bad, Its just I've been feeling sad." Said Noah.

"Oh Noah, I am so proud you have had the courage to recognise your emotions, now why dont we have dinner and talk about why you have been feeling this way." Said Noahs mum.
Joobi would you like to join us? she asked.
"SURE!" Joobi cheered. So off they went back inside to enjoy a meal together and share their feelings.

"Draw a picture that makes you happy"

The next day at school, Noah approached Miss Jubilee and said "im sorry i've been bad, its just i've been feeling sad."
"When I feel sad I like to draw pictures that make me happy" said Miss Jubilee.
"That sounds fun!" Noah cheered.
Miss Jubilee smiled and said "Well guess what? Today we are all going to draw a picture of something that makes us happy."
All the children cheered.

Noah didnt need Joobi anymore, he is much happier than before. Now Noah understands the motions to recognise his emotions and has since joined the schools council, where he shares the skill of understanding emotions and feelings.

Together with the help of his friends, family and school they all learnt the importance of recognising emotions, speaking about feelings and the importance of not judging one another.

Printed in Great Britain
by Amazon